MATT KENSETH

Midwest Sensation

by
Kelley Maruszewski

SPORTS PUBLISHING L.L.C.
www.SportsPublishingLLC.com

© 2003 Sports Publishing L.L.C.

Production manager: Susan Moyer
Project manager: Tracy Gaudreau
Developmental editor: Lynnette Bogard
Copy editor: Cynthia McNew
Cover design: Christine Mohrbacher

ISBN: 1-58261-653-1

SPORTS PUBLISHING L.L.C.
www.SportsPublishingLLC.com

Printed in the United States.

FOREWORD

I can't remember a time in my life when I wanted to be anything other than a race car driver. When I would begin winning in a series, I was always looking towards moving to the next level. Being part of a Nascar Winston Cup team was my ultimate goal. I am thankful to God, my dad, and all the team owners that were responsible for my success.

The 2002 season was great. Being consistent and finishing in the top ten in the point standings is important, but nothing compares to winning races. It is the ultimate feeling to drive that last lap around the track in front of 42 competitors.

As far as the future goes, I'm satisfied to keep doing what I'm doing. I'm living my dream. My goal now is to be competitive and remain in a position to win races. Do my goals including winning the Winston Cup championship someday? That would be more than I ever hoped for.

Matt Kenseth

Contents

Acknowledgments

My sincere thanks to my father, Roy Kenseth. He has always been full of encouragment and support for my brother Matt and me. Even though Matt's career choices probably were a little closer to his heart, he always made me feel equally important. His incredible scrapbooks of Matt's career were instrumental in making my first writing experience a smooth one. Thanks also to Matt for teaming up with me to make this an authorized biography.

The photography talent of Doug Hornickel is responsible for many of the great pictures. He has been taking pictures of Matt for twelve years. He also welcomed me into his home and encouraged me to choose whatever pictures I needed for this book. Thanks also to Jim Garrahan, Dave Drews, and Jeff Thompson for their photographic contributions.

Thanks to Rae Augenstein at www.mattkenseth.com for her research and for helping everything come together.

Finally, thanks to my friends Carrie Andersen and Pam Beyler for correcting my excessive use of commas before the editors did.

INTRODUCTION

Matt Kenseth represents the new generation of Winston Cup Drivers. Labeled the "Young Guns," they ride in and dominate races, find success on tough tracks without experience and mount threats for the Winston Cup championship. But being young isn't their only claim to fame. These drivers have an intense desire to win.

Their personalities are fiery. One is an open-wheel champ with a temper—another the son of an icon who built a racing dynasty, and has a taste for partying. But then there is Matt Kenseth. He is self-controlled and quiet. He is mature and witty. He is a good sport and a clean racer.

Matt is a role model for kids today. He is an example of success the hard way. Matt came from a small town, lived in an average house and did okay in school. Sacrifices were made and Matt made the best of every opportunity to break into racing.

Now, Matt is a superstar. Hundreds line up to see him at appearances—thousands join his fan club. He has hats and shirts with his name on them. He is a successful Winston Cup driver.

Matt's story could be yours.

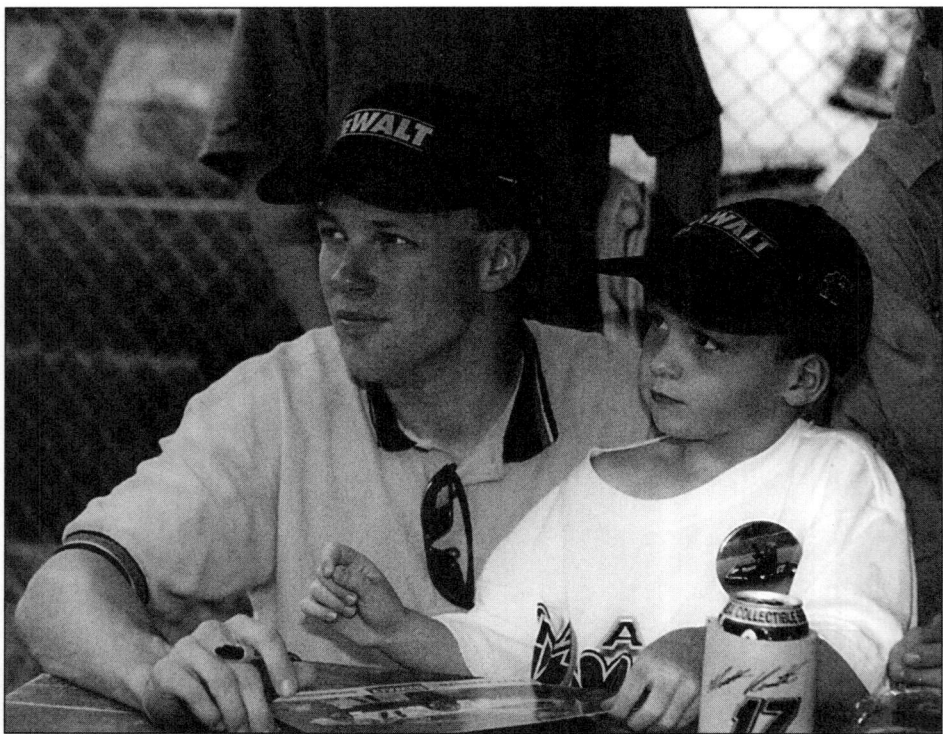

Matt and his son Ross enjoy a father and son moment.
(Photo by Doug Hornickel)

CHAPTER ONE

Small-Town Boy

Matt was born in Madison, Wisconsin, but it's only because Cambridge didn't have a hospital. The sleepy Midwestern town boasted fewer than 1,000 residents in 1972 when Matt moved in, and it hasn't changed much since. Born to Roy and Nicki Kenseth, Matt joined his sister Kelley in the family's home. Matt attended the local public school, played basketball, and was a good student. On Sunday after church, he may have taken a ride in dad's Corvette to McDonald's for lunch or stopped on the side of the road to pick wildflowers for his mom. Before cable TV, Gameboy and the Internet, the top entertainment of the day was Atari, and Matt mastered Asteroids and Missile Command. He lived a few blocks away from school, the park and the Methodist Church. His neighborhood was filled with children, and everyone played together. In the summertime, Matt and his friends would start some kind of project; whether they were building a raft to float down the Koshkonong Creek or constructing some sort of fort or hut with lawn chairs and blankets, they were always outside doing something. On summer nights, the kids would play basketball in the street or flashlight tag until their parents finally made them come in. If he had to be inside, Matt watched the *The Dukes of Hazzard*, built with Legos, or raced his dad on his slot car racetrack.

Matt's grandfather Helmer owned a Simplicity riding lawnmower, and Matt would walk the few blocks to his house to borrow it. In a small town, you could drive a mower down the street or

Matt rides a souped-up mower down Main Street in a local parade. (Kenseth family photo)

on the sidewalk, and people would just wave. It was a familiar sight to see Matt on anything with wheels or a motor. Whether flat-spotting the tires on his BMX bike or taking apart a mower engine to replace the gears (to make it faster, of course), Matt was content with his hands-on method of learning.

The racing bug bit Matt's father Roy in the late 1960s. He drag-raced at Great Lakes Speedway with his Camaro and later became interested in stock cars. Roy's three brothers all were similarly interested in speed and for a time raced competitively against each other. This Saturday-night hobby for the Kenseth brothers quickly became an obsession for Matt.

Finally the offer came. Like many fathers before him, Roy wasn't about to hand Matt a free pass to drive. "Matt," he decidedly began, "I think we

Matt plays football in his neighborhood in Cambridge. (Kenseth family photo)

ought to buy a race car, and I think I ought to drive it and you ought to work on it." When Matt turned 16, if he worked hard, he could take over the wheel. Soon Roy acquired a 1981 Chevrolet Camaro chassis for $1,800. This car would eventually carry Matt to his first victory at Columbus 151 Speedway later that July. One year later, Matt had earned a reputation as a phenom, stunning competitors and fans alike with wins at Columbus, the Dells, and Plover Speedways. With an ambitious attitude, he told the press, "I know it's way off, but I hope to race a super late model in ASA someday." He had spent the previous winter building a 1989 Buick Regal limited late model, outfitting it with a competitive motor and sporting a few sponsor decals. Unfortunately, the car's $20,000 price tag put a damper on the possibility of a father and son race team.

Stock car racing was a short-lived career for Roy, but it was not without its rewards. Roy won his first feature race at Jefferson Speedway, and his pit crew (Matt) was there to see it. After examining his wallet and Matt's natural talent, it didn't take Roy long to see that there was room for only one driver in this family.

Matt's sister Kelley, mom Nicki and Matt with their first race car outside the shop in May 1985. (Photo by Aren Larson)

Matt's first win in a fast heat, June 1988, Columbus 151 Speedway. (Photo by Dave Drewes)

CHAPTER 2

Midwest Roots

On Sunday afternoons, Matt would root for his favorite NASCAR driver, Dale Earnhardt. Then, father and son would head out to the shop and work on their car. Matt looks back fondly at his career beginnings. "I can still remember working in our little Rockdale shop—smelling the wood stove we used to burn to keep warm. Dad would stand in front of the wood stove while we worked. Mom would cook meals for all of us, and when I needed her to, she would sit in the car while I put it on the scales. That was always a good one."

Most of Matt's high school days were not spent at football games or dances and instead were spent in the little shop near the Kenseths' house. With a few buddies, Matt spent the next several years learning all about his race car, how to build it, how to fix it, how to pay for it, and how to win with it. Matt's dad recalls, "Matt wasn't shy about ordering the best and most expensive parts!" After graduating from Cambridge High School in 1990, Matt continued to live at home and began working as a technical assistant at stock car builder Lefthander Chassis in Rockford, Illinois. His job also included working on some of the cars and doing body work. Matt said, "It helped a lot because I learned more every time I worked on something. And when the new stuff comes out, I get to see it right away." He continued to compete in as many races as he could, moving up to the late model division. He won the

Matt is introduced at Rockford Speedway for the ARTGO All-Star 100, July 23, 1991. (Photo by Doug Hornickel)

season opener at Slinger and finished sixth in the overall point standings that year. This was the beginning of his presence as a winner and points challenger. Money and sponsorship were factors in the number of races Matt could run. He decided to focus on the ARTGO series, competed in the Red, White and Blue State Championship Series at Wisconsin International Raceway, and raced in the Miller Nationals at Slinger and in their Sunday-night points program.

Matt's goals had broadened since the previous year. Now he was saying, "I want to be a full-time race car driver. It doesn't matter on what circuit or what part of the country. My goal is to drive race cars professionally."

Many writers touted Matt's career, proclaiming, "It was never a matter of if he would win a major race, but when." One year later Matt stunned everyone and won an ARTGO race in his first visit to LaCrosse Fairgrounds. Matt was elated by the win. "I had no idea how many laps were left!" The team did not have the luxury of a two-way radio to communicate with the crew. Matt, only 19, was

Roy, Matt and long-time friend and crew man Todd Millard with an ASA entry in 1995. (Kenseth family photo)

the youngest driver to win. Suddenly the comparisons began. This youngster sure seemed a lot like the previous record holder, a skinny kid from Batesville, Arkansas who had previously taken the Midwest by storm—Mark Martin.

During the early '90s, Kenseth was becoming a household name in Wisconsin. Adding to his Rookie of the Year Titles at Slinger in '91 and then again at Kaukauna in '93, he wrapped up track championships in 1994 at both WIR (Kaukauna) and Madison International Speedway. 1994 also boasted a total of 18 late model feature events and the Miller Genuine Draft Nationals title. In '95, he won races and championships. He found success with Fred Neilsen and competed in a few ASA races, hoping for television coverage.

Matt had conquered the Midwest. Now the question was where to go from here.

VICTORY!!! July 1994. (Photo by Doug Hornickel)

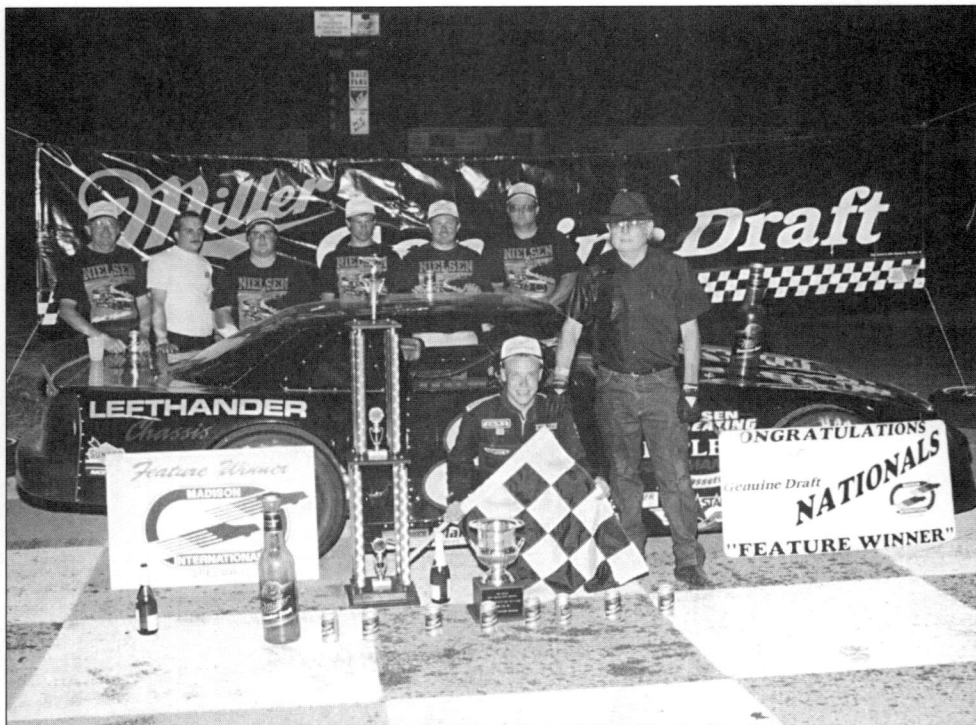

Matt and car owner Fred Nielsen win the Miller Nationals.
(Photo by Doug Hornickel)

CHAPTER THREE

Moving Down South

It's not that Matt wasn't content living at home with his parents. But Rockdale just wasn't a mecca for stock car racing. He had covered the field at the Wisconsin tracks, and he had his hopes set on the southern home of racing, North Carolina. Even though Matt had experienced success in the Midwest, the paychecks always disappeared into more equipment. He was pretty much broke when he loaded up some furniture in his stock car trailer and moved to Huntersville.

He planned to join Carl Wegner and run for the Hooters Cup championship, not to mention plans to include select NASCAR All-Pro events and five races in both NASCAR Busch and SuperTruck divisions.   Matt held his own against the rough cut of drivers on the Hooters menu and managed to achieve his first victory in Anderson, South Carolina.   In May of 1996, Matt made his Busch Series debut at Charlotte in an unsponsored car rented from Bobby Dotter.   He was satisfied with staying out of trouble and finished 31st.   He still entertained hopes of additional Busch races, but lack of sponsorship and financial hardship forbade it.

Despite Matt's determination to put down roots in the south, he was lured to Wisconsin in 1997 by Gerry Gunderman.   Gunderman owned a well-established ASA team, and Matt was ready for a full-time shot at the ASA circuit.   He relocated to

Matt waits in line to qualify for the ATRGO Dixieland 250 at WIR, Kaukana, August 6, 1991. (Photo by Doug Hornickel)

Milwaukee and began building cars. Their first outing was in Kenly, North Carolina, where Matt finished second. Before Matt left the track, he received a career-changing phone call.

Matt wins his first Hooters race in Anderson, S.C. (Kenseth family photo)

Kenseth family photo

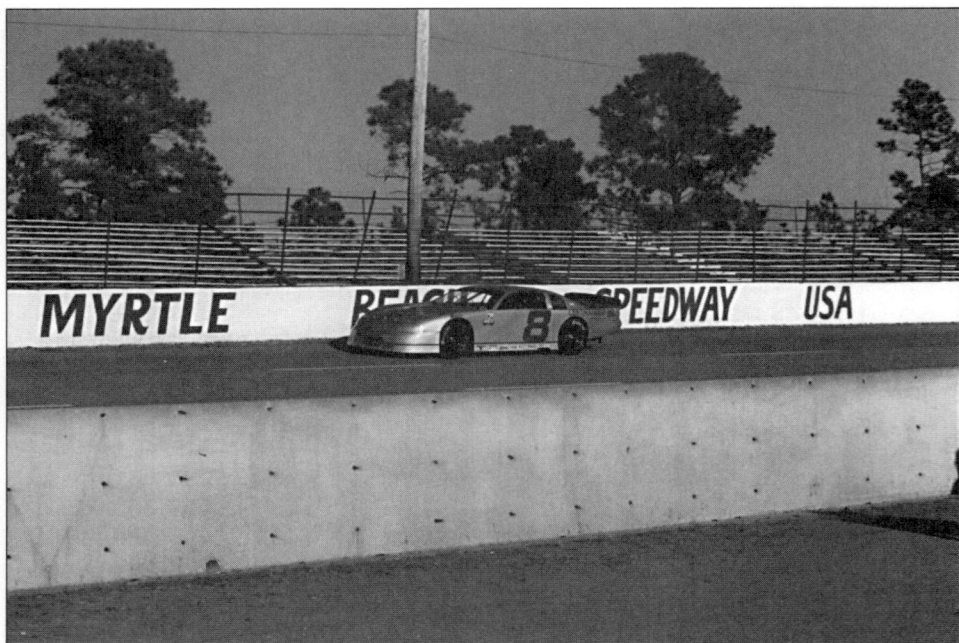

Matt at Myrtle Beach, December 1995. (Kenseth family photo)

Friends & Rivals

Some of the headlines in '93 looked like this:
Kenseth Nets Race, Reiser Gets Title;
Kenseth Tops Reiser in WSTS Finale; Kenseth
Holds Off Reiser; Kenseth Wins WSTS Final, Reiser
is Series King. Robbie's and Matt's relationship on
the track was purely competitive. They were both
there to win. While competing in the Wisconsin
Short Track Series, during the season finale Kenseth
won his first 200-lap race, and Reiser scored the
series title. Reiser's title earned him the use of an

ASA car and hauler for the '94 season, but Robbie's sights were set higher, on Busch Grand National racing. It would be three years before Kenseth and Reiser would join forces, leave their rivalry behind in Wisconsin, and form an alliance that would last for many years to come.

Reiser struggled on a limited budget and began to compete part-time in the Busch Grand National Series. Soon after, he realized that acting as crew chief and driver was time-consuming and nearly impossible. He opted for crew chief, and in 1997 secured driver Tim Bender and a full-time sponsor in Kraft Singles. After Bender suffered a neck injury in Bristol, Kenseth found himself the recipient of a surprising phone call. Robbie's decision to call had been based on their past competition. Matt had been riding out the Wisconsin weather in an ASA ride with Gerry Gunderman and faced a troubling decision. Reiser was offering a six-race deal, maybe enough to get Matt noticed on the NASCAR circuit, but it meant walking away from a commitment and a promising season in ASA. After weighing the options, Matt again turned his future to the south.

Matt in the #8 car and Robbie Reiser in the #71 as on-track rivals in 1993. (Photo by Doug Hornickel)

Matt's first appearance with the team was at Nashville Speedway. He qualified third and finished 11th. The next race was his first superspeedway start. Matt finished seventh at Talladega. In July, the team returned to its home state of Wisconsin, to the Milwaukee Mile. Matt suffered a potentially dangerous crash there during the morning practice

Photo by Jeff Thompson

when the throttle stuck and he took a path straight for the wall. Luckily, Matt was not injured. They qualified with a backup car, finishing a respectable 12th. Matt's best finishes of the year were placing third at both Dover and California.

Robbie and Matt prerace at the Milwaukee Mile, July 6, 1997. (Photo by Doug Hornickel)

Robbie and Matt on pit road at the Milwaukee Mile. (Photo by Doug Hornickel)

As the season drew to a close, Kraft Singles announced that they would not be returning in 1998. Even though the team's financial future hung in the balance, Matt found Robbie knowledgeable and easy to talk to. Robbie's experience as a driver helped cement this new relationship between crew chief and driver. They completed the 1997 season with two top fives and seven top tens and a second-place finish in the Rookie of the Year standings.

Matt and Mark await driver introductions at Atlanta Motor Speedway, November 2001. (Photo Kelley Maruszewski)

Family and friends cheer Matt on at the Milwaukee Mile. (Photo by Kelley Maruszewski)

✠ Little Help From My Friends

It's hard to say just what caught Mark Martin's eye. The comparisons began when Matt erased Mark's name from the record books with the ARTGO win in 1990. They also shared a history of racing many of the same tracks in the Midwest. More importantly, Mark, mentored by Wisconsin legend Dick Trickle, had also unsuccessfully tried to enter the BGN series, only to be plagued with financial problems, and eventually retreated to ASA. Or maybe Mark noticed the same thing many others saw in Matt: unbridled talent. Matt recalls, "I guess he likes the way I drive. It's a little overwhelming to be working with him. Mark is someone I always looked up to."

Martin approached Kenseth after a drivers' meeting at Talladega earlier in the spring of '97 with an offer to test with him later that year at Darlington. It was here that Matt had his first opportunity in a Winston Cup car and where the beginnings of a solid friendship with Martin were formed. That day, Matt found himself chatting about chassis setups with Mark while running some nonrecord-breaking speed laps at the Lady in Black. By the time Matt's first season in the Busch Series concluded, he had secured a "five-year testing contract" with Roush Racing, as well as Roush's interest in helping Reiser Enterprises and Matt secure Busch sponsorship for 1998. Mark would continue to be pivotal in Matt's career for the next several years, speaking up for the budding star and opening the door for endless opportunities to learn.

In the early days, Matt felt more like a Mark Martin fan than a future teammate. On a break-

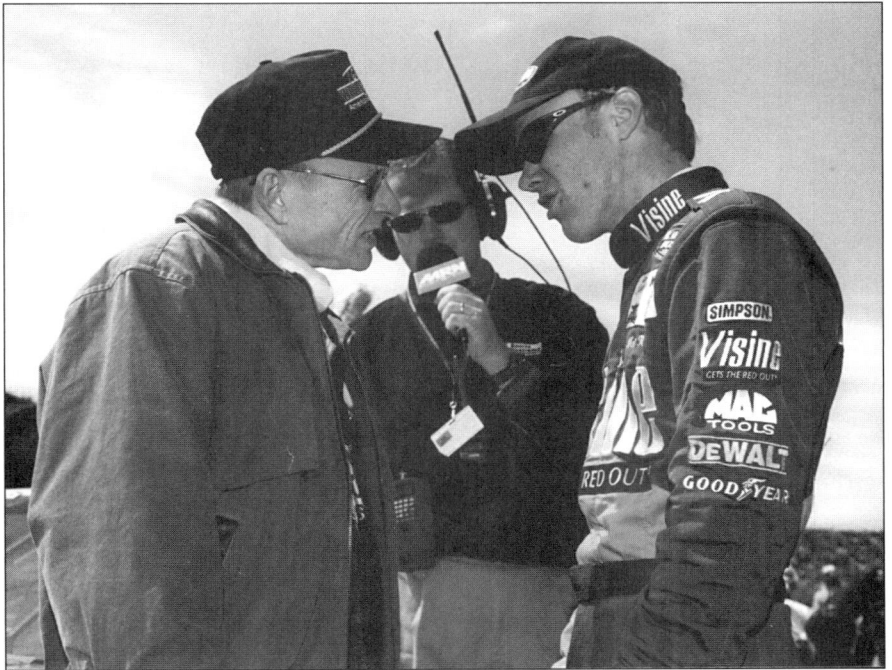

Matt and Mark Martin compare prerace notes on pit road, March 2000. (photo by Doug Hornickel)

fast outing, Matt remembers, "Mark couldn't even eat his eggs. There were so many people looking at him and coming up to talk to him." Mark began to influence Matt in off-track practices such as the importance of a regimented physical workout and eating only healthy food. Their sons were also close in age, and both were interested in go-kart racing.

Mark's wisdom sometimes came off in the form of humor towards Matt. When Matt bumped Mark off the pole for a Busch race in Atlanta, Mark called his lap "young and dumb." Mark would go on to win the race, but Matt finished second, the only car even close to challenging Mark for the win.

Mark Martin was listed as car owner along with Jack Roush when Matt took the DeWalt Tools-sponsored Ford Taurus for its five scheduled runs in 1999. A fall schedule including Michigan, Darlington, Dover, Charlotte and Rockingham would be Matt's final practice before bidding for Rookie of the Year honors in 2000.

Although Mark would always remain a mentor and teacher, his intensity towards his own racing career eventually limited the time Mark and Matt spent together.

Mark Martin, #60, leads Jeff Burton, #9, and Matt, #17, during the Busch race at Darlington Raceway. (Photo by Doug Hornickel)

Photo by Doug Hornickel

CHAPTER SIX

Busch Breakthrough

The 1998 season began with one goal: winning races. Matt would compete in the 31-race Busch Grand National schedule. In Daytona, Reiser Enterprises was prepared to announce their primary sponsor when the whole deal fell apart. It looked like the end of the road, until a midnight meeting secured Lycos, an Internet search engine, for a one-race deal. A day before the race, a NASCAR official accompanied Reiser's Chevrolet out of the track to have it painted black and to have

*Driver introductions at the Milwaukee Mile, July
1998. (Photo by Doug Hornickel)*

the decals applied. Despite their sixth-place finish
at Daytona, the next week at Rockingham the blue
and red car with a yellow 17 sported only a small

*Matt's first Busch Grand National win at Rockingham,
February, 1998. (Kenseth family photo)*

Lycos decal on its rear quarter panel. The decal was meant as a thank-you and perhaps enticement into further sponsorship. Throughout the running of the Goodwrench Service Plus 200, the driver of the 1998 Chevy was referred to several times as "Robbie Reiser," but in the last few laps there was no confusion as to who was driving. Tony Stewart was bumped up out of the groove, opening the door for Kenseth. Crossing the finish line was a monumental occasion for both Robbie and Matt. The 25-year-old midwesterner from Cambridge, Wisconsin, with only 24 Busch Series starts, came out on top. He stood on top of his unsponsored car with a logo-free blue driver's suit and the points lead to boot. Matt was ecstatic. Tony was not. "You've got to do what you've got to do," Matt reported.

Matt's dad was there to relish his son's first victory. When Roy returned to Cambridge, there were hand-painted signs in business windows and "Congratulations Matt" lettered on the bank marquee.

Mark Martin finished third and congratulated Matt in victory lane. Mark then paid him the ultimate compliment when answering a question about his relationship with Matt during an online chat. He stated, "Matt is a superstar in the making. He is a tremendous driver, and if somebody said, 'Why don't you create from scratch the ultimate race car driver?' That's the one." When two-time Busch Series champion Randy LaJoie was asked to name his competition for an upcoming race at Darlington he mentioned Mark Martin, Jeff Burton, and Tony Stewart. But, he went on to say, "Matt Kenseth—oh, my gosh—he's good." Matt basked in the glory of his victory; it was well earned.

A few weeks later, Lycos signed on as the primary sponsor for the remainder of the season. It was only a few months later that they began to reap big dividends. On June 14, Matt started on the pole and won his second BGN race, the Lycos.com

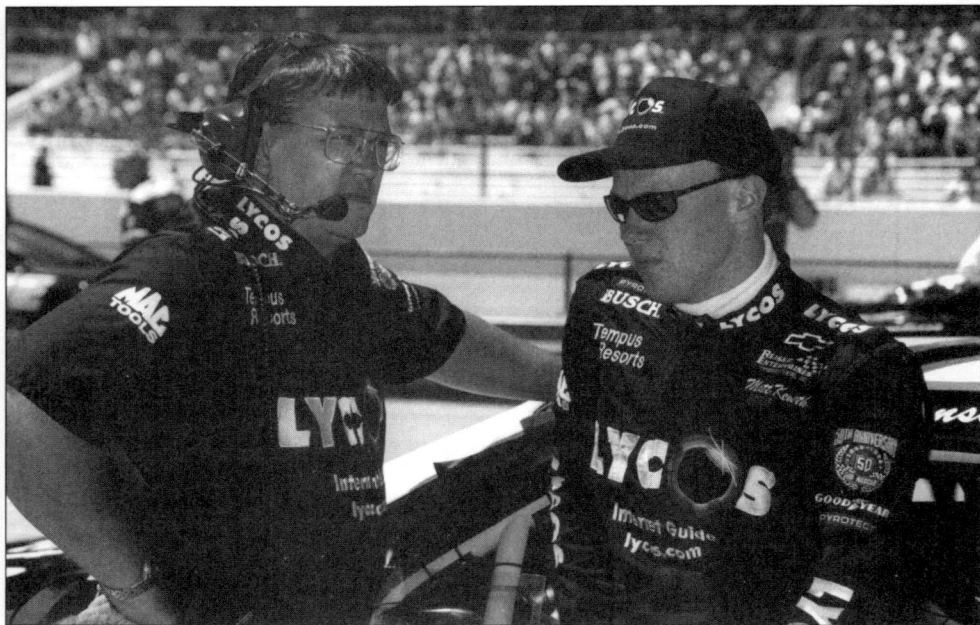

Photo by Doug Hornickel

250 at Pike's Peak International Raceway, and he regained the series points lead.

Competition in the Busch Series was at a peak. Steve Park, 2000's Rookie of the Year, had fared well as a newcomer and had also raised the bar for future performances by Tony Stewart, Dale Earnhardt Jr. and Matt Kenseth. Seasoned veterans like Randy LaJoie, Elton Sawyer, Mike McLaughlin and Todd Bodine, along with Winston Cup regulars Mark Martin, Bobby Labonte and Jeff Burton, kept the competition lively. But by the end of 1998, the Busch Series had become Matt Kenseth vs. Dale Earnhardt Jr. The two had become friends, and there was rarely an interview or article that didn't mention the two synonymously. Additionally, they were door to door or fender to fender in most of the Busch races. As the '98 season began to wind down, Junior was in the points lead and Matt was in hot pursuit. After race number 31 was complete, Matt had posted three wins, 17 top fives and 22 top tens but fell 48 points short of champion Dale Jr.

The 1999 season opened up fresh possibilities: a rematch with Dale Jr., and a new sponsor, DeWalt Tools. Ironically, Matt's first BGN win of the year came at Darlington in March. A Winston Cup stand-in job for injured Bobby Labonte followed that Sunday, where he finished 10th. Matt and Junior remained neck and neck throughout the season, with Jeff Green becoming a strong contender. The media continued to surround the son of Dale Earnhardt and his greatest challenger. As their relationship on the track heated up, tempers flared when Junior wrecked a dominant Kenseth at Dover. Their schedules were filled with interviews, appearances and the newfound responsibilities as-

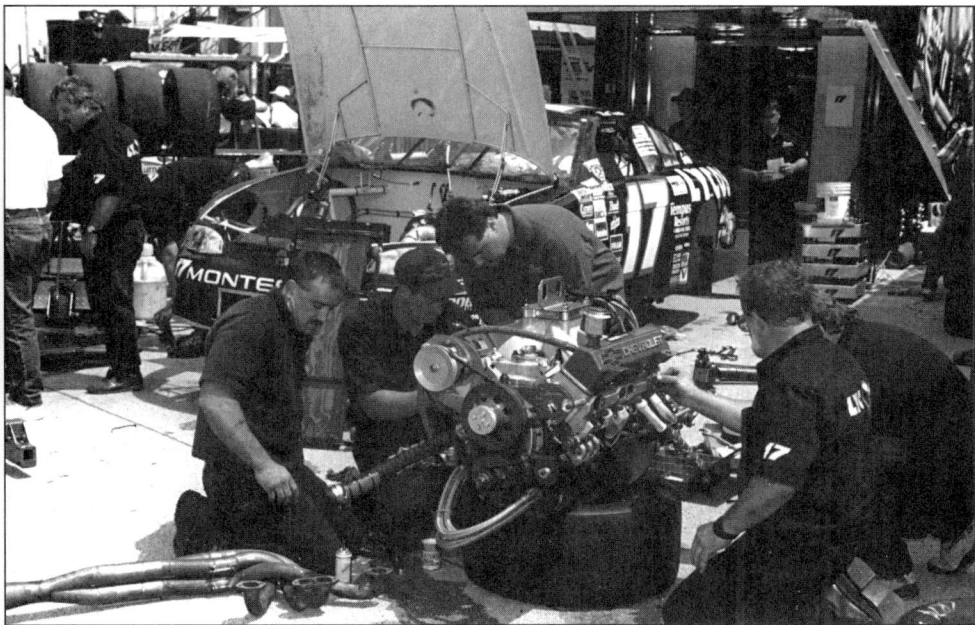

Photo by Doug Hornickel

sociated with making the move to Winston Cup. Dale Jr. was fast becoming NASCAR's bad boy, while Matt appeared to be more stable and mellow. Despite a mutual respect for each other, their days of "hanging out" were diminishing.

By September, their statistics were nearly a mirror image, each driver claiming 17 top tens, 13 top fives. Junior edged by Kenseth with five wins to Matt's four. Twenty-six points separated the two from a championship.

Roy Kenseth and Matt celebrate Matt's first BGN win.
(Kenseth family photo)

*Substitute driver Kenseth at his first Winston Cup
drivers introduction. (Photo by Jim Garrahan)*

Hold the Fries

Moments after Matt cashed in his third Busch victory at Dover in September 1998, he jumped into a Winston Cup car. He had been testing Cup cars for months with Mark Martin, but this was neither a Roush Ford nor a test. It was Happy Hour—Winston Cup practice for the MBNA Gold 400 scheduled for Sunday. Bill Elliott's father had passed away the previous day, and while searching for a replacement for Elliott, Martin suggested Kenseth. Crew chief Joe Garone and team manager Mike Beam had not even met Kenseth. However, less than 24 hours later they would be communicating like a veteran team. Matt qualified 16th, ran in the top five most of the day, and at one point was in second place behind the eventual race winner Mark Martin. Matt recalls, "The only time I got emotional was when I passed Rusty Wallace. Mark was the only car in front of me. Then I got a little goofy for a few laps and thought about catching him."

Matt was colorful in every way that Sunday. Elliott's McDonald's Ford was sporting a special tie-dye Big Mac paint scheme, and Matt was wearing a matching driver's suit. Matt was right in the sponsor groove when radio traffic picked up this conversation with crew chief Garone. Garone asked his driver what he needed during an upcoming pit stop. Kenseth replied, "I need some water, don't need any adjustments on the car…and hold the fries." On another humorous exchange, Matt smoked the tires leaving pit road and radioed in, "Sorry for the John Force exit, boys."

Matt gets a few last-minute instructions on pit road before making his Winston Cup debut. (Photo by Jim Garrahan)

It was quite a change for Kenseth, who spent most of his Sundays on the couch watching Cup races. When asked about possibly being intimidated by the NASCAR regulars, Matt replied, "I'm a racer. I race as hard as I can. That's just the way I'm built and that's the way I was raised." The praise was unanimous from fellow drivers and teams. Rusty Wallace referred to Matt as "talented and smooth," and Joe Garone said, "He's just really smart, kept really calm and cool. He just did a great job." The media attention carried over into the next day. Matt's phone rang continually with congratulations and job offers from car owners. Despite the persuasiveness of the offers, Matt remained loyal to mentor Mark Martin and his contract with Roush Racing.

Matt's sixth-place finish was the best debut performance by a driver in a Winston Cup Series race since Rusty Wallace finished second at Atlanta on March 3, 1980.

Photo by Doug Hornickel

Photo by Doug Hornickel

CHAPTER EIGHT

Rookie of the Year

Ready or not, here we come! 2000 marked a year of young guns waiting to make their mark on the veterans of NASCAR's premier division. Seven rookies would contend for the Rookie of the Year title, and everyone looked to the son of a legend to walk away with it. Tony Stewart had outdone all expectations with three wins in his rookie season in 1999. Now the rookie class of 2000 was under pressure to win out of the box. Matt chose, in addition to running a full Winston

Cup schedule, to continue to race in the Busch Series. Visine had joined forces with Reiser Enterprises, and a 20-race schedule had been assembled with some of the previous Busch series crewmen and a new crew chief. Matt used four fresh tires as pit strategy and drafting help from Joe Nemechek to cement his first win at Daytona and create a record three top ten finishes in three starts. It was Matt's eighth Busch win in 86 races.

Matt's Winston Cup DeWalt team was solid. With Robbie Reiser as crew chief, several crewmen who had moved up to the Cup series from the Busch leagues, and two years of experience, the Dewalt team was beginning to reap dividends. Teammates Jeff Burton, Mark Martin and the rest of the gang at Roush were contributing as well. However, when Dale Jr. scored his first win in a Cup race at Texas and then duplicated his efforts at Richmond, the pressure for Matt to win increased.

Matt at Darlington, 2000. (Photo by Doug Hornickel)

Matt took advantage of the Burton brothers' late-race spins in Fontana to chalk up his second Busch victory of the year. The following Sunday, it looked as if he would pick up his first Cup win at California, as well. After leading over 100 laps and dominating the second half of the race, a late race caution shook up the field and squelched his bid for victory. Matt was disappointed. "I sat there all day and planned on losing because I just knew something was going to happen. The minute we were home free, sure enough there was the yellow." The consistent Reiser and Kenseth chose to take four tires instead of two and were mired too deep in traffic to reclaim a higher position than third. Jeremy Mayfield won, but Kenseth came out of the shadows, proving to be more of a threat to win now more than ever.

The DeWalt crew measures up during prerace inspection. (Photo by Jim Garrahan)

Coming into Charlotte in May, Matt and Dale Earnhardt Jr. were both running in the top 15 in points and competitively performing each week. Junior turned heads and had crowds roaring with his free-for-all victory at the Winston, where he picked up the pole position for Sunday night's Coca Cola 600. But the "other rookie" would shine in NASCAR's longest race.

Photo by Kelley Maruszewski

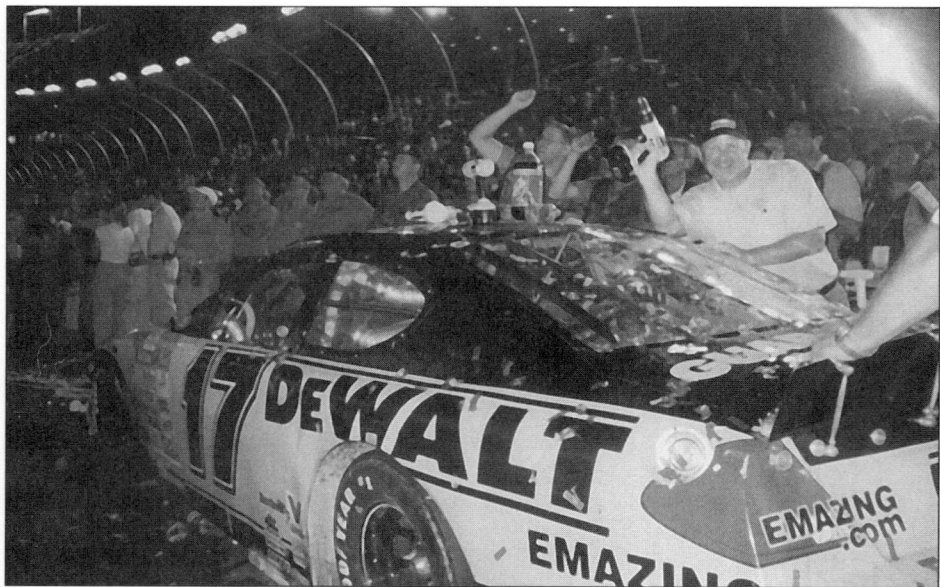

Celebrating Matt's win at the Coca-Cola 600. (Photo by Kelley Maruszewski)

CHAPTER NINE

Rain Delay

Most NASCAR drivers make their home in the Charlotte, North Carolina area. Midseason they settle down to spend a good chunk of time at Lowe's Motor Speedway in Concord. After the Winston weekend, the qualifying and practices stretch from Wednesday through Saturday. Sunday night is a long time coming, but the atmosphere under the lights with 185,000 fans all waiting to spend their night with screaming tires and revving engines gives it an enticing flavor.

The night was rainy, halting the race partway through and holding it up for about an hour. But the crowd waited and watched bids for the lead as Dale Jr. and Jerry Nadeau both ran well early that evening. Nadeau had engine problems and Junior had pit stop problems. Fortunately, Matt Kenseth would have no problems. "My heart started beating pretty hard as soon as I took the lead from Bobby," recalls Kenseth. Running a clean and smart race, as the last laps were ticking off Matt glanced in his rear view mirror. It was still full of Bobby Labonte, one of the Winston No Bull competitors who would receive an additional $1,000,000 for a win. Tonight it was Matt's turn. When he crossed the finish line, flash bulbs flickered, fans cheered, the DeWalt pit crew went airborne from the pit wall and a 28-year-old rookie driver who was not a good ol' boy and was not Dale Jr. elated everyone with his stunning win. Seconds later the DeWalt Ford tore through the infield grass, spraying water and sod in a true celebratory style. When Matt got out of his car to face the press, he could not hide his emotion. A win at Charlotte in his 18th career start. How did he pull it off? By racing the same way he does every race, every week. "I can't believe how good the race car was. I was using the tires up pretty hard to keep Bobby behind me. I didn't know if he was saving his car or not, but I was going as hard as I could," Matt told reporters.   In victory lane, Matt was joined by his fiancee Katie, crew chief Reiser, Mark Martin, Jack Roush, and later was doused with a water bottle by Junior. The DeWalt crew had been redeemed after its struggles the previous week during the Winston. Their pit stops were flawless. Diligence had paid off. In addition to the excitement of the win, Matt remained

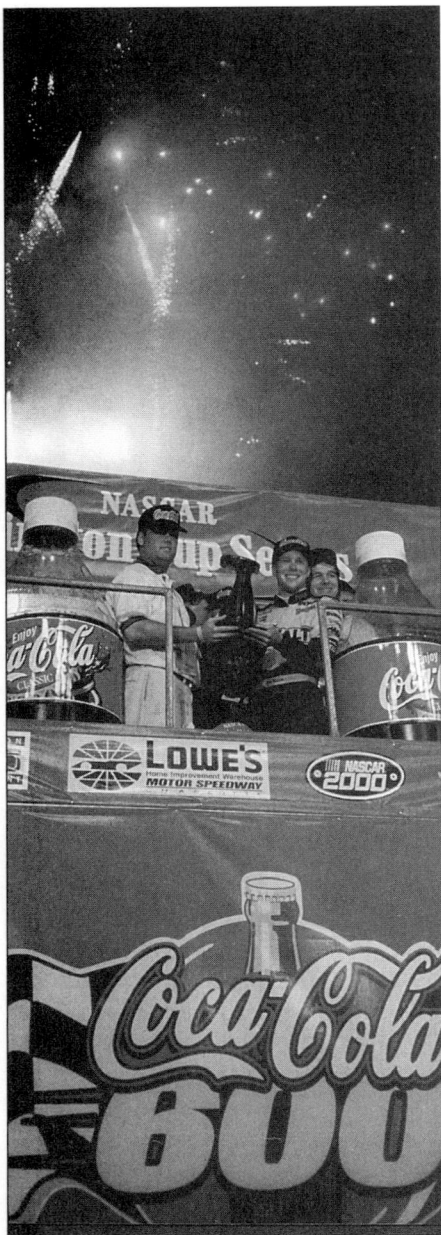

in the points lead in the rookie battle. Although Junior had more wins, Matt was becoming known for his consistency. Matt had come from a 21st-place qualifying effort to win NASCAR's longest race. He was the only driver outside the top 20, not to mention the only rookie, to ever clinch a Coca-Cola 600.

Photo by Kelley Maruszewski

Matt continued to mow down the competition in the Busch series, winning back-to-back races at Dover and Charlotte. Double duty, racing both Busch and Winston Cup, is more than a full-time job. But Matt methodically ran his races, and as his first full season in Winston Cup drew to a close, he had not relinquished his lead in the rookie battle. Just like math class, the rookie points system is just a little harder than it has to be. Even though Matt had more "points," NASCAR still had the right to award the title to a competitor, based on wins, on- and off-track attitude and the like. Since Dale Jr. had been the obvious favorite, Kenseth fans waited to see if Matt would receive this prestigious award.

In December 2000, Matt attended his first Winston Cup banquet in New York and was presented with the Raybestos Rookie of the Year Award and a check for $50,000. Matt's season may have paled in comparison to Junior's victorious romps, but the level-headed, steady-handed Kenseth's season was a victory as well.

Matt capped off his 2000 season by marrying his best friend, Katie Martin. The two had met at a mutual friend's wedding and had been together ever since. Matt and Katie were married in Wisconsin, and then a few weeks later made an appearance at the Matt Kenseth Fan Club's First Annual Party. Over 1,000 fans turned out to congratulate Matt on his Rookie of the Year title and recent marriage.

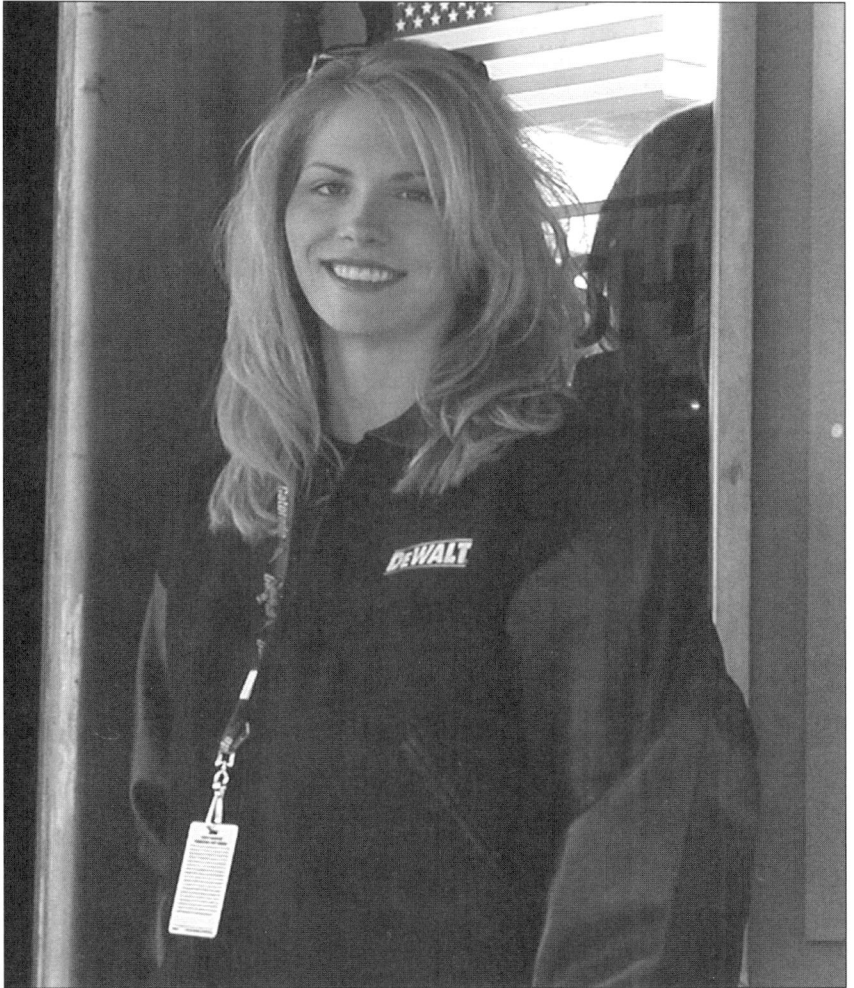

Katie Kenseth (Photo by Rae Augenstein)

Matt and Dale Earnhardt, Jr. (Photo by Doug Hornickel)

Sophomore Jinx

As the countdown to Daytona 2001 began, the spotlight again shone on Matt and Junior, this year pitted against each other as potential Winston Cup champs. Rookies Casey Atwood, Kurt Busch, and Jason Leffler would be hard-pressed to achieve the friendly rivalry and celebrity status that the previous year's candidates possessed. Matt would again be pulling double duty, racing twenty Busch Grand National races in addition to his full Winston Cup schedule. The DeWalt car sported a special all-yellow paint scheme with the Raybestos Rookie of the Year logo emblazoned on the hood. NASCAR history was forever changed that day when on the last lap of the Daytona 500, Dale Earnhardt's Chevrolet slammed head on into the outside wall of the Speedway. A few hours later, a dark cloud settled over the NASCAR community. Matt had always known that in the game of high speed and chance, danger lurked in the shadows. It could have been anybody. It could have been him.

Despite low spirits the following week at Rockingham, 43 drivers started their engines. The feeling in the garage area of the tight-knit community was closer than ever. Each driver and crewmember honored the memory of Dale with a black hat bearing the familiar #3. Dale Jr.'s life and career had taken a different turn. Finally a separation was forged between the comparative paths of Matt and Junior.

Dale Jr. went on to have a banner year, winning restrictor plate races and finishing eighth in points. But troubles plagued Kenseth and the DeWalt team, from blown engines to broken rear end gears. In Atlanta, one of Matt's favorite tracks, the motor blew and sent Matt hard into the wall. The car was engulfed in flames. Matt made a quick exit, able to effortlessly release himself from the now-required HANS safety device. Goodyear had come out with a much harder tire, and the team's inability to compensate for its handling differences only added to their problems. Even though the engine department was showing improvement, the Roush drivers still paled in horsepower in comparison with giants Yates, Penske, and Hendrick. As if that wasn't enough, bad luck and bad weather also affected the

Photo by Doug Hornickel

team. They used 11 provisionals, and their average starting position was 27.8. Matt was vocal about his disappointment in being unable to run up front and contend for wins. Rumors were beginning to surface about an unsatisfied Matt leaving Roush. It was a difficult year.

Near the end of the season, Matt's luck began to turn around, and Matt posted three fourth-place finishes in the last six races. In October, the DeWalt pit crew won the World Pit Crew Championship at Rockingham, breaking the old record with a 17.695-second stop. Morale began to improve, and Matt statistically finished one position better (13th) in the final point standings than he had the previous year. Matt's final Busch series standings were impressive, with one win at Bristol, six second-place finishes, 12 top fives and 14 top tens out of the 24 races in which he had competed in.

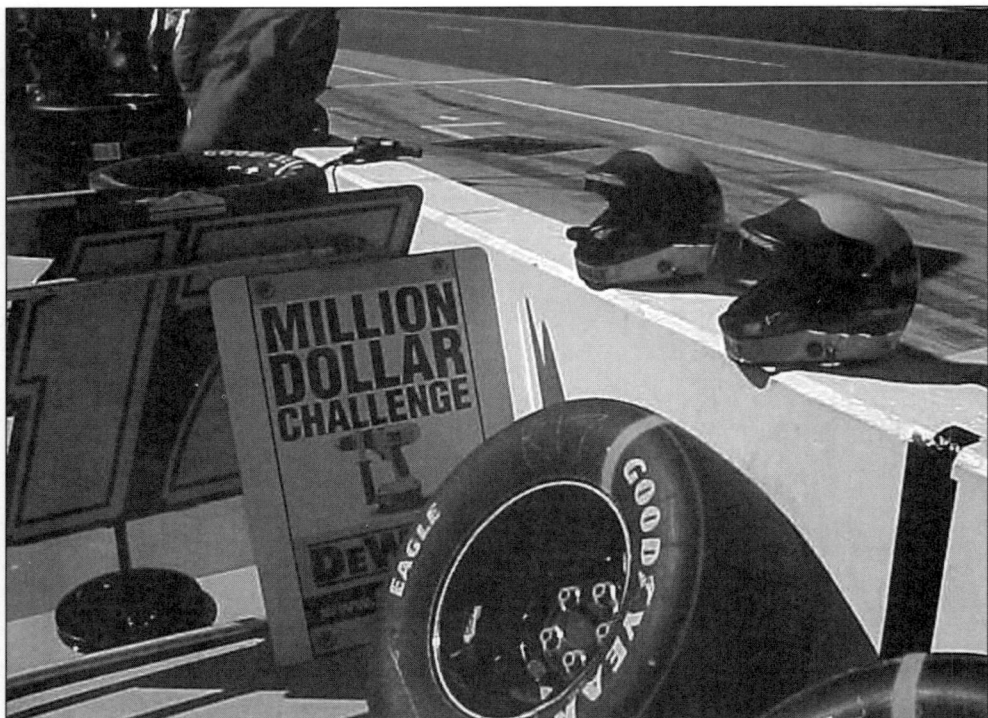

DeWalt's Million Dollar Challenge pit box and pit road at Las Vegas Motor Speedway in 2002. (Photo by Kelley Maruszewski)

Championship Contender

Momentum. That's what every driver strives for. It's the force that pulls out the best of the previous year and plugs it into the brain when encouragement is needed. The DeWalt team was oozing with momentum, and the team members were fired up and ready to get back to racing. Daytona is a wild card, and sure enough Matt was caught up in the "big one." He began his season with a 33rd-place finish and 33rd in Winston Cup Series points. The following week at Rockingham,

Matt qualified 25th and showed strength early in the race. He led laps, gained positions in the pits, and was running a smart race. The track surface at Rockingham is a tire shredder. Even after a few laps on "stickers" (new tires), lap times fall off nearly a full second. When a late-race caution flew, Ricky Craven stayed out on old tires, and the leaders, Labonte, Marlin and Kenseth, all pitted. When the laps were coming to a close, Marlin and Labonte both slid up the track, and Matt made the winning pass inside both of them. A spin would bring out the last caution flag of the day, and while cleanup ensued, the red flag was not thrown and Matt took the checkered under the yellow. It was a huge win for the DeWalt team. They had been down, but they would not be beaten. Matt had taken himself a piece of the "Rock" as he had done four years ago in his first Busch series victory.

The fanfare died down, and later that evening Matt and his wife flew back to Wisconsin to be with Matt's father as he underwent surgery for prostate cancer. Matt walked through the door of the Kenseth home with a Winston Cup Series hat with the race date embroidered on the back and the Subway 400 trophy for his dad. The best postrace interview was done that evening on the couch between father and son.

The following week, Matt was the center of a media blitz in Las Vegas. He had qualified for the Winston No Bull Million last season in Talladega, and DeWalt had prepared to launch a $1,000,000 promotion. A wild spin through the infield grass and a loose-handling car produced a 17th-place finish. A few weeks later, Matt went from worst to first at Texas. The DeWalt team fought mechanical issues with their engine, and the penalty for changing engines prior to the race translated into a 43rd-place starting position. He had finished eighth or better in the last four races. The following week produced a second-place finish at Martinsville. Matt proved able to overcome adversity when he raced back onto the lead lap at Richmond and finished sixth, as well as when a cut tire and a well-timed caution brought him to a second-place showing at Charlotte.

The team had pulled together. Quick pit work earned Matt his first Winston Cup pole position and $50,000 with a 13.23-second pit stop at the Winston. Midway through the season, Matt was a solid second in points. Matt's crew was again credited with top-notch pit work when a last-minute "gas and go" put Matt in the lead at Michigan with nine laps remaining. NASCAR threw the red flag with five to go, but Matt opted not to pit and held off challenger Dale Jarrett for win number three.

When Richmond rolled around again in September, Matt was again plagued by tire troubles. Despite going a lap down each time he got a flat tire, the cautions fell in his favor, and he was twice able to race back onto the lead lap. It was a stunning victory. Kenseth managed to encompass both

Matt, Tony Stewart and Dale Jr. play blackjack for the Vegas "No Bull" promotion. (Photo by Kelley Maruszewski)

ends of the spectrum with 16 top ten finishes, but also nine finishes of 30th or worse. He remained the winningest driver, but was too inconsistent to tame the points system.

When Matt did experience trouble, he was running up front. At Sears Point he suffered a broken gear while running third, and at Pocono a second-place run was thwarted by a broken transmission. During the fall race at Charlotte, Matt was in contention for the win when he experienced his first engine failure of the year. At Rockingham, the DeWalt pit crew for the second time won the Pit Crew Championship.

As his banner season was coming to a close, Matt secured his fifth win of the season at Phoenix International Raceway. It was an emotional victory for Matt, who had become a frequent visitor to victory lane. The last race of the year was at

Homestead. Tony Stewart and Mark Martin were cemented in the top two positions, but fewer than 100 points separated positions three through eight. A good run for Matt could have put him as high as fourth, but due to an engine failure Matt finished eighth in the final point standings with five wins, 11 top fives and 19 top tens.

What will the next chapter hold in the continuing saga of Matt Kenseth? Will 2003 be the year for a Winston Cup Championship? Whether feast or famine, be sure that Matt will remain competitive, clean, and cool.

Matt Kenseth Fast Facts

Birthdate: March 10, 1972

Birthplace: Madison, Wisconsin

Residence: Mooresville, North Carolina

Family: Wife Katie, Son Ross, Cat Lars

Favorite Race Track: Dover Downs

Hobbies and Interests: Snowmobiling, Video Games, Motorcycling, Boating

Favorite Band: Metallica

Favorite Sports Team: Green Bay Packers

Personal Vehicles: 2002 Roush Stage 3 Mustang

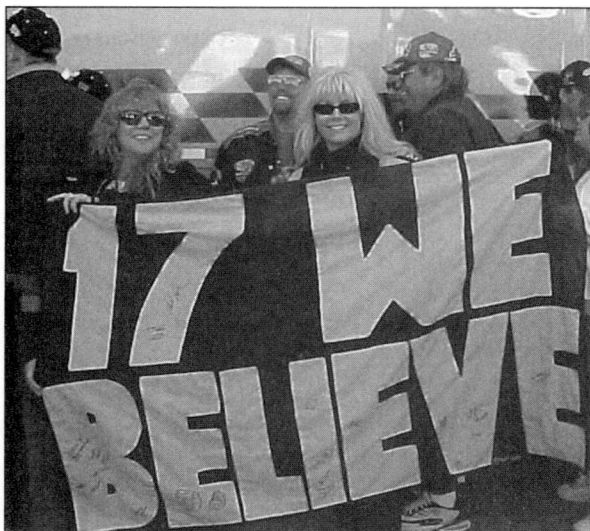

Matt's fans let him know they were behind him by toting this banner to every race in 2002. (Photo by Kelley Maruszewski)

Matt Kenseth Fan Club Information

Matt's Fan Club was formed by his father, Roy Kenseth, in 1997. Based in Matt's hometown of Cambridge, Wisconsin, the fan club expanded from the Kenseth living room to a storefront with memorabilia, merchandise and one of Matt's early Busch Series race cars.

2003 Fan Club members receive an autographed 8x10 hero card, membership card, credential/ticket holder, stickers and quarterly newsletters. If you would like to join the Matt Kenseth Fan Club, please send $20 ($15 + $5 S&H) to: MKFC, 10 Water Street, Cambridge, WI 53523, or you can join online at www.mattkenseth.com.

"I really like to see the kids out here as race fans. That's what means the most to me, I guess, is when we get to do appearances and autograph sessions. It's great to see the kids and try to be somebody that they can look up to."

Matt with Chelse Lindenbaum and Taylor Bogard at The Matt Kenseth Fan Club Dinner, December 2002. (photo by David Bogard)

About the Author

Kelley Maruszewski is the newsletter editor and owner of the Matt Kenseth Fan Club. Along with her husband Mike, they operate Matt Kenseth Fan Club Headquarters in Cambridge. When she's not turning out newsletters or watching her brother Matt race, she spends her time homeschooling her two children Amber and Evan.

She began writing in the late 1980s for a local entertainment newspaper, where she contributed rock band interviews, movie and book reviews, and the paper's first article on racing, about "Matt the Brat." Although she never pursued a career in writing, when she heard a children's book about Matt was in the works, she asked for a chance to write it.

Her lifetime goal is to see Matt win at every racetrack. So far she's scratched Charlotte, Phoenix and Richmond off her list.